Sacajawea

The Journey West

To Mayo, who rides like the wind, just like Sacajawea.

ISBN 0-590-47898-2

Copyright © 1994 by Don Bolognese and Elaine Raphael.
All rights reserved. Published by Scholastic Inc.
CARTWHEEL BOOKS is a registered trademark of Scholastic Inc.

12 11 10 9 8 7 6 5 4 3 2 1   4 5 6 7 8 9/9
Printed in Singapore
First Scholastic printing, November 1994

Sacajawea

The Journey West

By Elaine Raphael and Don Bolognese

Cartwheel
B·O·O·K·S ®

Scholastic Inc.

New York Toronto London Auckland Sydney

Mountain Home

"Wake up little sister."
Sacajawea opened her eyes.
Her older brother, Cameahwait, was smiling down at her.
"I have a surprise for you," he said.
A pinto pony stuck its head into the tepee
and poked Sacajawea with its soft nose.

"He is a beauty," she exclaimed as she stroked his smooth mane.
Later Sacajawea climbed onto the pinto's back.
"Now let's see how fast he is."
Her brother jumped onto his horse, too.
Together they galloped through the camp
and out into a meadow.

The Hunt

In the winter, Sacajawea's people
lived on the high plateau.
In the spring, when meat was scarce,
the Shoshoni left their mountain camp
to hunt for buffalo.
They traveled many days across the great plains
in search of a buffalo herd.
Other tribes watched them.
They wanted the Shoshoni horses.

Finally, a Shoshoni scout spotted a herd of buffalo.
The Chief, Sacajawea's father, sent all the men to the hunt.
On his way out of camp, Cameahwait called out to Sacajawea.
"I will bring you back many buffalo — be careful, and
watch for raiders."

Capture

While the women and children waited for the men
to return, they worked and sang songs.
Sacajawea was picking berries when suddenly a
distant sound made her stop. She looked up.
Were the hunters returning so soon? she thought.
"Raiders! Raiders!" her mother cried out.
Horses and men cut through the camp.
Sacajawea ran toward her horse.
A raider crossed her path.
He reached down, grabbed her around the waist,
and pulled her onto his horse.

Sacajawea was ten years old when she was
taken from her people.
She never saw her mother and father again.

Slave

Sacajawea became a slave to the Minnetaree raider
who captured her.
She lived in his lodge and worked for his family.
She carried in water and wood.
She pounded corn into flour. She scraped hides
and sewed them into leggings and moccasins.
In the growing season, she worked from morning to night
in the corn fields.
She missed her people.
She wondered if she would ever see them again.

Three years later, she was sold to a French-Canadian fur trader who lived among the Minnetaree.
At the age of thirteen, she became a wife to Toussaint Charbonneau.

Captains Lewis and Clark

In the winter of 1804, a group of explorers came to
the Minnetaree village.
They were on their way to the western sea and needed
someone who could speak to the horse people, the Shoshoni.
When they heard about Sacajawea, they hired her and her husband.

The leaders, Captains Lewis and Clark,
spent the winter months preparing for the journey.
The expedition was ready to leave in the spring, after the river ice melted.
The two captains, with Clark's servant York,
stood in the bow of the first boat.
Beside them, with her baby, Pomp, was Sacajawea.
Four summers ago, I was taken from my people, she thought.
Now I am taking my son home.

The Missouri

Weeks passed.
The expedition had traveled hundreds of miles.
One evening, Sacajawea and Captain Clark
climbed a hill above the river.
The setting sun lit up the wide, muddy river
as it crossed the rolling plains.
A large herd of buffalo raised dark clouds of dust.
Sacajawea pointed to the distant mountains
that stood out against the sunset.

"There, far away, beneath the shining mountains, is my home.
The meadows, the horses, my people. They wait for me."
She spoke in Shoshoni.
Captain Clark did not understand her words.
But he saw that she was happy.

The Expedition

The journey was not easy.
The days were hot; the nights cold.
Sometimes, the men had to pull their boats with ropes.
Other times, they carried them up rocky banks
and over thorny ground.
The men suffered cuts and bruises and insect bites.
Some had colds and fever.
Sacajawea felt ill, too, but she didn't complain.

She pulled thorns from the men's feet.
She bandaged their wounds with medicine
she made from herbs.
When their food was gone, she found roots for them to eat.
At night, she mended torn clothes
as they sat around huge fires built
to keep wild animals away.

The Sickness

One afternoon, after a heavy thunderstorm,
the expedition stopped to make camp.
They all sat by the fire to dry out their clothes.
Sacajawea's body ached. She began to shiver.
By evening, she was in great pain.
She had a high fever and was very weak.
Everyone was worried.
York made a lean-to and put her to bed.
Captain Clark mixed sulphur water with medicine
and gave it to Sacajawea.

He whispered to her, "We are close to your people, Sacajawea. You must get well."
He held her hand as she fell into a deep sleep.
The night passed.
The day dawned, clear and warm.
Sacajawea opened her eyes.
Her fever was gone.
She smiled at Clark and at York, who was holding Pomp.

The Shoshoni

Early one August morning,
Sacajawea put on a new buckskin dress
and tied a beaded belt around her waist.
She put red paint on her face and hairline
and drew a circle on each of Pomp's cheeks.
"Our people are close; they will know us by these signs,"
she said to her son.
Suddenly she saw riders coming toward them.
They rode beautiful, painted horses with feathers
    in their manes.

The riders stopped and looked at her.
Sacajawea began to sing. She danced, and pointed,
and sucked her fingers.
"What are you doing?" Captain Clark asked.
"What does it mean?"
"These are my people. The people I eat with,"
answered Sacajawea.
The warriors sang their greeting song as they circled her.
"Tonight we will be with my people!"
she shouted with joy.

The Meeting

Sacajawea walked barefoot into the Chief's tepee
to join the others.
The Chief began by smoking a pipe.
When the Captains, too, had smoked, the Chief began to speak.
He spoke slowly to Sacajawea, so she could translate his words.
She watched him and, as she listened, she began to remember
a voice saying, "Wake up little sister."
Suddenly, Sacajawea cried out.

"Cameahwait — my brother!" She wrapped her blanket
around her brother and began to cry.
The Chief, too, was moved to tears.
"I thought I would never see you again," he said
as they held each other.
After a while, the Chief spoke again.
He agreed to help the expedition.
The captains would have the horses they needed to cross the mountains.

Farewell

After a few days among the Shoshoni, it was time
for the explorers to leave.
Sacajawea turned to look at her people.
Her brother rode up beside her.
Slowly she folded her hands across her chest.
It was the Shoshoni sign of love.
Cameahwait reached out and touched her hand.
Captain Clark gave a signal, and the horses
and men began moving.

Ahead were many dangers, steep rocky trails, narrow paths,
and sudden snowstorms.
But Sacajawea was not afraid.
She turned her horse toward the mountains.
My work is not finished, she thought,
And I want to see the great ocean.

Drawing America

You can draw Sacajawea and what she saw on her journey. On the next few pages we have drawn pictures for you to copy and color. Copy the drawings freehand — or use the guidelines we've drawn. Here's how:

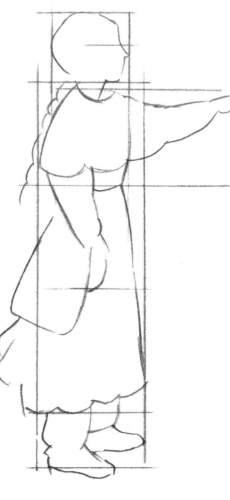

1. Copy the guidelines first. Ours are blue to make them easier to see. Use an ordinary pencil and ruler.

After putting in the guidelines, draw the main outlines of the figure, one box at a time.

2. Next, add details like the fringe and decorations on the dress. Take your time and copy one section at a time.

Watercolors and colored pencils were used to color these pictures. The same technique was used to do the illustrations for the story of Sacajawea.

3. Erase the pencil guidelines. Now you are ready to color.

4. Although Captains Lewis and Clark and their men were in the army, they often wore frontier outfits made of buckskin and fur. On special occasions they put on their army uniforms.

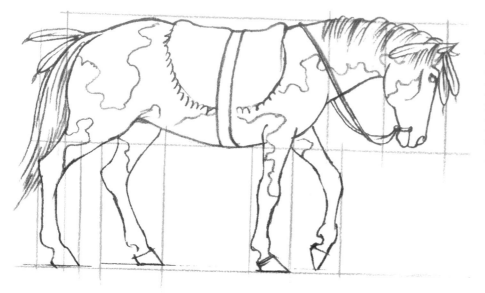

The Shoshoni people raised horses. One of their favorite types was the pinto. The Shoshoni liked to decorate their horses with paint and eagle feathers. Often the painted markings were symbols of old battle wounds or protective animal spirits.

The saddle was a piece of buffalo hide. The bridle was a rope tied around the horse's lower jaw.

You can color the horse to look like the pinto in this picture or make it solid brown, black, or white. Look at the illustrations throughout this book for more ways to color horses.

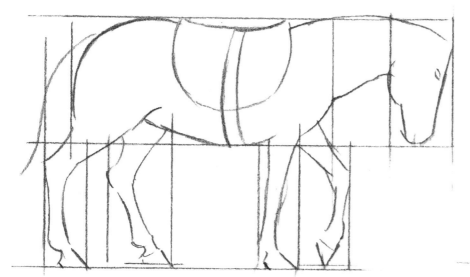

The tepee was the most common dwelling of the Plains Indians. The tepee was easy to put up and could be taken on journeys when the tribe searched for buffalo. The covering of the tepee was usually made of animal hides. The Shoshoni people sometimes covered their tepees with mats woven from branches.

Sacajawea was captured by the Minnetaree Indians (also known as the Hidatsa Indians). They lived in a part of the United States known as the Great Plains.

Some of the Native Americans who lived on the plains moved their camps in order to follow the buffalo herds.

Other tribes, such as the Minnetaree and Mandan, had permanent villages with farms on which they raised corn, squash, and beans. They also hunted buffalo.

These pictures of a Mandan chief and a Minnetaree buffalo dancer are copied from paintings by Karl Bodmer, who visited and painted the Plains Indians in the 1830s. Some of the Indians who posed for him were alive when Lewis and Clark and Sacajawea were there.

This Minnetaree warrior is dressed for the buffalo dance. There is an easy way to draw his mask. You will need tracing paper and a dark pencil.

Notice that the dancer's shield is symmetrical. Draw it the same way you draw the mask.

1. Take a whole sheet of tracing paper and divide it in half. Copy half of the buffalo mask on the right side of the paper.

2. Fold the paper along the center line. Put the folded paper on a table. Make sure the right half (which has your drawing on it) is facedown.

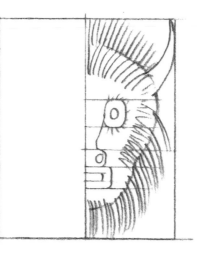

3. With the left half facing up, your drawing will show through onto the left half of the paper. Use your pencil to trace your drawing.

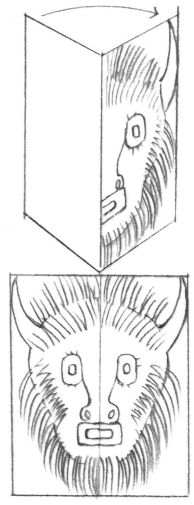

4. Open your paper. Now you have a whole buffalo mask.
You can use this trick anytime you want to draw something that is symmetrical — the same on both sides.

A Note from the Authors

In November, 1805, Sacajawea and the expedition reached the Pacific Ocean. They decided to build a fort and stay there until the following spring. In August, 1806, the explorers returned to the Minnetaree village they had left sixteen months earlier. That is where Sacajawea and Charbonneau decided to stay.

Captain Clark offered to educate Sacajawea's son, Pomp (who was called Jean Baptiste by his father). Five years later the boy went to stay with Clark in St. Louis. Pomp grew up to be a guide to western travelers.

There are some historians who believe that Sacajawea died in 1812, but there are others who claim she lived until 1884.

Throughout history, Sacajawea's name has been spelled several ways. When it is spelled *Sacajawea* it means "boat launcher" in the Shoshoni language. But when it is spelled *Sacagawea* or *Sakakawea* it means "bird woman" in the Minnetaree language.

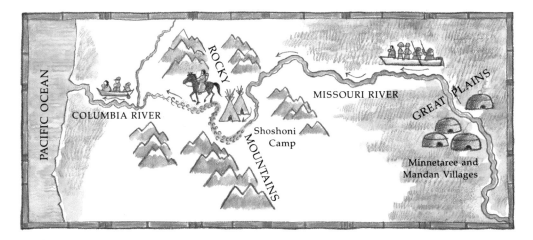

This is a map that shows Sacajawea's journey west from the Minnetaree village to the Pacific Ocean.